CURIOUS CORNWALL

Michael Williams

BOSSINEY BOOKS

First published in 1992 by
Bossiney Books, St Teath, Bodmin, Cornwall.

Typeset and printed by
Penwell Print Ltd, Callington, Cornwall.

ISBN 0948158 77 8

ACKNOWLEDGEMENTS
Front cover photography: Roy Westlake.
Other photographs: Ray Bishop; Alex Gardiner; Felicity Young.
Front cover design: Maggie Ginger.

'... IN THESE stones, something of themselves ...'

About the Author and the Book ...

MICHAEL WILLIAMS, a Cornishman, started full-time publishing in 1975. He and his wife Sonia live in a cottage on the shoulder of a green valley just outside St Teath in North Cornwall.

In addition to publishing and writing Michael Williams is a keen cricketer and collector of cricket books and autographs. In Cornwall he is a Patron of the Broomfield Horse Sanctuary at Penzance. In 1984 he was elected to The Ghost Club and remains convinced Cornwall is the most haunted region in Britain.

His contributions to the Bossiney list include Paranormal in the Westcountry, Superstition & Folklore *and* Supernatural Search in Cornwall.

Now he explores Curious Cornwall. *'Curiosity', he says, 'like beauty, is largely in the eye of the beholder. The selection here, of course, is highly personal . . .'*

CURIOUS CORNWALL

THE CORNISH are a curious race and Cornwall is a curious land. The landscape and the waters that lap around the rugged coastline stir our curiosity.

'Curiouser and curiouser!' cried Alice.

Did Lewis Carroll ever come to Cornwall?

Collins English Dictionary is a good friend, never far from my desk. I turned to page 366, and found *curious* had as many as five sections. I liked the third section: 'interesting because of oddness or novelty; strange, unexpected.' But a sentence or two of warning before we begin this exploration across *Curious Cornwall*, we are using the word as a broad umbrella, and here, in Cornwall, things are rarely black or white, rarely clear-cut. In a way, Cornwall poses more questions than it answers. Often in looking for a solution, we find another query – and maybe that is why Cornwall is such a curious and beautiful place.

Cornwall remains essentially Nonconformist – and not just in politics and religion. Cornwall has often gone against the tide – and will continue to do so. It is no mere accident the Cornish language is alive and Cornish nationalism stirs in hearts and minds.

Maybe it is all to do with the Devil.

Some say one day the Devil came to the eastern bank of the Tamar. Standing there, rubbing his chin and looking across the ribbon of water to Cornwall, he considered carefully.

'No,' he finally decided, 'I won't risk it. Yonder every person is made into a Saint, and everything into a squib pie, I don't feel qualified for either position.'

That, of course, is just a good story, but C.E. Vulliamy, touring

THE POWERFUL Cornish seas stir the emotions and the imagination.

Cornwall in the 1920s researching his book *Unknown Cornwall*, may have come to the heart of the matter when he found himself among the abandoned primitive villages and stone circles out on the Cornish moors. '*Time suffers a contraction,' he wrote, 'you realize that you are close to the ancient builders, that the "old people" have left behind them, in these stones, something of themselves . . .*' Seventy years after Vulliamy I know precisely what he means. Who can walk across the bleached grasses of a Cornish moor, wind in his or her face, and not feel related to earlier events?

In the year 1914 a fisherman out on Bodmin moor encountered a Moorland man who was quite unaware of the fact that we had been at war with Germany for more than two months!

Denys Val Baker, a Celt from Wales, was fascinated by the mystery and magic of Cornwall. Back in the 1950s in a chapter entitled *The Magic of Cornwall* he told this illuminating story:

'The very long ago! How much it has been impressed and impregnated into the granite body of Cornwall, how much it remains alive, a part of the daily life. Once when climbing to the top of a hill above St Ives, a man said to a little boy: "This was where the Druids worshipped their idol gods." When the boy asked "How long ago?" the man replied vaguely, "About a hundred years ago, I s'pose." Past and present, moments and centuries, all are entangled and interwoven in Cornwall. Eternity is contained in a hundred years.'

Perhaps the Cornish landscape and the strength of the atmosphere – very powerful in places – combine in working on us in a highly individual, almost eccentric way. The steamroller of dull conformity has not yet crossed the Tamar.

Curiosity too is a fascinating characteristic: a quality which drives the individual on to creativity and invention – or disaster – and sometimes all three.

I therefore happen to think *curious* is a fine word: when for example I include sections relating to Cornish churches and inns, I am not implying these hostelries or places of worship are either odd or strange – merely that they have some aspect or feature worthy of inclusion in this curious catalogue.

'THE CORNISH landscape and the strength of the atmosphere …'

Fashion and fad, prejudice and preference, time and neglect all help to define what is a curiosity and, just as important, what is not. Curiosity, like beauty, is largely in the eye of the beholder. The selection here, of course, is highly personal and only representative. To embrace all the curiosities of ancient Kernow, you would need a thousand pages – and still offend by omission. Generally too I have steered clear of subjects covered in earlier Bossiney titles.

Ronald Duncan, a writer who was born with a silver spoon in his mouth, lived and farmed high on the North Cornwall-Devon border. He once told me 'A true autobiography would never find a publisher, and if it did, it would never hold a reader. To record accurately we would have to write most of our lives on water.'

In his brilliant autobiography *How to make Enemies*, published in 1969, he reflected: '*So when we write our life we falsify it . . . If a man lives twenty-five thousand days or so, how many of them can he remember? Not more than a couple of hundred at the most. But the rest were days he lived: they fell like leaves trodden under . . .*'

On this exploration across *Curious Cornwall*, I find quite the reverse. Cornwall is littered with strange facts and facets. I am writing these lines on the shoulder of a green valley in North Cornwall.

Across the valley is the village of St Teath. '*The name is pronounced to rhyme with death,*' was how Sir John Betjeman put it. Sir John knew the shade and subtlety of Cornwall. Back in the 1600s St Teath was the home of Anne Jefferies who performed miraculous cures – people came from miles to see her. Of Anne's healing, Sabine Baring-Gould reflected: '*. . . they are to be put in the same category of faith cures all the world over, whether performed at Lourdes or by the Christian Scientists, or by the Shamans in the Steppes of Tartary.*' She never charged a penny and some say she was fed by the fairies. Was she a witch of a saint? Three and a half centuries on, we shall never know the answer.

From our garden we can see Delabole Quarry. More than 500 feet deep and over a mile in circumference, Delabole is the only example of large-scale quarrying outside North Wales and the Lake District. Ronald Duncan, who on occasions said some harsh things about Cornwall and the Cornish, always wrote beautifully; he got to the soul of Delabole in three simple sentences; '*There is no inscription on a slab of Delabole. It bears no silly rhyme or motto, or any mark of this*

THE FORMER Poet Laureate Sir John Betjeman 'who knew the shade and subtlety of Cornwall.'

DELABOLE SLATE Quarry: an old photograph of rare large-scale quarrying.

or any age. It is what it is, and in its primeval remoteness it makes a comment on what we are.'

Nearby is the hamlet of Helstone. An authority on the occult tells me a ley line runs right through it. Our knowledge of earth energy culture stems from China where the art of divining the earth energies, flowing along the leys – the dragon paths the Chinese call them – helps decision-makers know where best to build a temple or a house: a location which harmonises with the flow of energy from the earth.

Then on December 16 1991 Cornwall achieved a real 'first' when a commercial wind farm – the first in Britain – went into operation just outside the village of Delabole. So today Delabole is pioneering a greener and safer world – and one day those white windmills, thirty metres high, will become antiques. Now *there* is a curious thought.

Come then, let us begin our journey across *Curious Cornwall.* I promise a fascinating expedition as we travel from page to page – and place to place.

OLD PICTURE POSTCARDS OF CORNWALL

PICTURE postcards have come a long way – a long way in time and terms of geography.

In 1869 one Dr Herman persuaded the German government to produce a card the size of an envelope with a writing area to contain not more than twenty words – Europe had its curious rules and regulations even then.

The penny post brought written contact within the scope of every family capable of reading and writing. Previously letter writing was an expensive business – you paid according to distance and the number of sheets of paper used – consequently letters were a matter for the rich or those engaged in commerce.

The passion for collecting picture postcards – like so many things – began in Victorian times, and the Queen herself was a collector. The Victorians also had this delight in keeping records and scrap books. People suddenly began using postcards as a rapid, reliable and cheap method of sending a brief message. It is extraordinary that in those seemingly leisurely days you could send a card late in the afternoon announcing your arrival at a certain destination on a certain train next day, knowing the card would arrive first. Many, who met friends and relations or paying guests at, say, Penzance station, would have been informed this way.

It is only in comparatively recent years that old picture postcards have attracted the eagle eyes of the dealers – reminding us that fashion and the passage of time shape curiosities – and antiques. Now we find cards, which many of our grandparents threw into the dustbin or put on the bonfire, are appearing in sales and antique shops. Those cards which survived have now become real collectors' items.

Indeed collecting picture postcards has become the third largest collecting hobby in Britain today, only surpassed by collectors of stamps and coins.

In this chapter I have harvested some old cards from Cornwall, especially for this publication. Looking at some of our Cornish cards, it is incredible to reflect how some locations have changed *almost* beyond recognition whereas other places retain the physical personality – the atmosphere – of generations ago.

Some cards here date back to the early days of the century; others are about fifty years old. They are records of a vanished or vanishing Cornwall.

WHERE BETTER to begin our nostalgic trip than Land's End? These visitors, of course, would see vast changes at Land's End today. There are more buildings and greater tourist facilities, but for those who wish to absorb the remoteness and the old magic of Land's End, all you need do is walk a few furlongs and you'll discover that the beginning and the end of Cornwall can still be a refreshing renewing experience. Mind you: Dr James Whetter and his Cornish Nationalist Party would not approve of the sign in our postcard referring to the 'first and last refreshment house **in England.**' *He and his colleagues would say 'England ends on the eastern bank of the Tamar.'*

SEAGULLS remain part of the Cornish scene. Here an old picture postcard shows a brace of gulls airborne at Treyarnon.

SEASIDE HUMOUR frequently featured on old picture postcards. Here is a delightful example from Bude: four kittens all accommodated in boots. This is an especially interesting card in that inside the flap are as many as 11 photographs of places in and around Bude: Nanny Moore's bridge, the breakwater, the bathing pool and, of course, the Bude Canal. This kind of card was known as a 'mailing novelty' – its shape having been passed by the GPO for printed paper postage rate – the stamp costing just a half penny.

HERE IS a delightful card from Polperro. The property on the left is known as Jews House. Dick Jolliff, a retired Polperro fisherman, told me a local man had gone around giving various properties picturesque names 'to add a little colour to the Polperro scene. Dick reflected: 'You don't find many Jews in Cornwall ... they find the Cornish tough opposition!'

A GRACEFUL line of swans at Looe.

HERE is a magnificent Cornsih character; a fish wife. The card is dated September 16 1903, and addressed to a lady living at 7 Morrab Road, Penzance. A.M.P. who sent the card penned only ten words 'Just a card for your Collection, With Love.' I guess this Cornish fish wife was photographed scores of times by early visitors to Cornwall, and if she came from Newlyn she may well have been painted by one of the Newlyn School of Painters who frequently used local people as their models.

BY CONTRAST, for some the Edwardian days were a chapter of elegance as this old postcard implies – a lady, dressed with style, about to uncork a splendid bottle of champagne. The Edwardian who bought this card would be astonished to know is has gone up at least 200% in value! Tony Bates of King Street Curios, Tavistock, a specialist in old postcards and cigarette cards, says 'Only about 10% of the cards originally published have survived.'

SLAUGHTER BRIDGE, just outside the town of Camelford. Within the context of King Arthur, Camelford has always been a favourite in the search for Camelot. You can rarely see the glory of a bridge merely by standing on it. Look at Slaughter Bridge from a neighbouring field and you will understand it's really ancient, not arched but built over flat stones on piers, rather like that splendid clapper Postbridge on Dartmoor. There are bigger, more beautiful bridges, but Slaughter has a character of its own.

This is an essential part of any Arthurian tour of Cornwall, for it strides the River Camel in its infancy, and the Camel hereabouts is often said to have been the site of the Battle of Camlann.

Malory told the dramatic tale of Arthur's final battle when he was forced to fight his bastard son Mordred who had betrayed him. A furious conflict – in the end only two of the knights of the Round Table were left alive. Arthur knew his time had come. 'I am come to mine end,' he said and he slew Mordred with his own spear, but the dying traitor raised his sword and struck his father on the head piercing through the helmet to the brain. So Arthur had killed Mordred with his own hands, as he had sworn to do.

Upstream in a nook lies the stone, embroidered in moss and strange lettering, called Arthur's Grave but it is almost certainly that of another Celtic Chieftain. And if the stone slab here does commemorate some historic battle, it is more likely to have been one fought in 825 during the Saxon conquest of Cornwall.

TWO CARDS which relate to one of my favourite Cornish towns: St Ives. My maternal grandmother was a Rosewall, once a well-known and prosperous St Ives family. So ancestry may partly explain my affection for this lovely corner of Cornwall. At the height of the season it's often a congested place, but, out of season, St Ives retains her essential quality – and qualities. The Digey was probably photographed out of season long ago. I wonder about the boy photographed at Hicks Court. Was he just passing by or did he earn a few coins by posing there?

▶

ANOTHER PIECE of beautiful photography at Bude, showing the Harbour and Summerleaze. This card was posted in the summer of 1906.

THE EARLY photographers captured a Cornwall that has gone for ever – many of them were really artists. Here is such a case; a magical scene entitled 'Leaving Harbour, Boscastle.'

TWO LADIES above a natural arch at Lundy Cove. This card is dated August 17 1933 and was despatched from Padstow, addressed to a lady living in Hornsey, London.

THE PASTY is not only a Cornish curiosity, it is a part of Cornish history. Marika Hanbury Tenison, who wrote and broadcast about cooking with such eloquence, told me she arrived in a remote mining area of South America and was greeted by a Cornishman. 'Just in time for crib,' he said, and gave her and her party tea and pasties. 'If you are Cornish,' he said, 'you have to have your pasty a day to keep you going.'

RECALLING A ROMANY WAY OF LIFE

CORNWALL has the ability to spring surprises. That fact is underlined by the National Museum of Gypsy Caravans at Tereife Park, just outside Penzance, and its very presence here in Cornwall is due to the vision and enthusiasm of one man. Tim Le Grice, a local solicitor, has long had an interest in Romanies, their life style and history. His interest, combined with his passion for horses, fired him to establish the museum alongside the stud farm and horse sanctuary.

The Le Grice family has lived at lovely Trereife House for nearly three centuries. The first member to live here was Charles Valentine Le Grice, descended from one of William the Conqueror's men who came over in 1066.

The range and diversity of the exhibits is remarkable because traditionally, when a gypsy died, his or her caravan was burned. However Tim Le Grice was lucky that he was able to acquire a collection of Romany caravans in Pembroke.

Gypsies, of course, have long been associated with fortune telling. The truth is man has always been curious about his future, wanting to 'see' ahead, to control his destiny and usually multiply his fortune. This and their reputation for the gypsy's curse and, in olden days, a certain amount of crime meant they were viewed with deep suspicion by non-Romanies. Even in the reign of the first Queen Elizabeth repressive laws were passed and, for many years, simply being a gypsy was a crime – and punishable by death. Moreover if we come forward to this century, we find Hitler persecuted the Romanies and the Jews with equal and brutal fanaticism.

It is ironic that many thousands of gypsies lost their lives in Hitler's

THE OPEN LOT or Yorkshire Bow, probably built for summer use at the fairs.

concentration camps on the orders of a man who depended on the astrologers. Most people today accept the fact that we owe our modern forms of divination to the gypsies, particularly Romany women. But they are more than perceptive, many excel in music and languages and various manual arts and crafts – and they have a language of their own. They came to Europe somewhere in the 1400s – and their language adds weight to the belief that they came from India.

Going into the Museum at Trereife can be a curious experience. You not only step back in time, but into a vanished Romany way of life. The audio-visual show has an almost haunting quality. The old

A YOUNG Romany with pet dog – a display photograph at the Museum.

A SQUARE Bow waggon built by William Wright around 1907. This was the only Square Bow waggon made by the accomplished builder – his waggons became a status symbol for Romanies.

ALEX DRAPER, a current traveller in Cornwall.

photographs – and how well those early photographers froze some magical moments of gypsy gatherings and camp fires – bring us in touch with ancient culture. The sound effects are especially poignant: the hoof beats on the road, the creaking of the waggons, the turning of the wheels, the voices and the laughter all take us from the here and now into another world. There are also excellent examples of Romany craft: artificial flowers and corn dollies, wooden pegs and utensils.

The greatest glories of the museum are inevitably the waggons. It was not until the last century that the travellers replaced their tents with caravans made of softwood – making them light for travel. The horse was a key character in their life style – and there was considerable respect for the animal. Interestingly even today, in an age dominated by the motor car, the horse is often still with Romany people.

Some magnificent restoration work has been carried out on the waggons by Terry Ansell of Ashton near Helston. Terry, who often works on site at the museum, specializes in building, restoring and painting gypsy waggons.

A concession to the motor car is the fortune teller's caravan, built by the Eccles Caravan Company, about 70 years ago, which would have been towed by a diesel or steam vehicle in the late 20s or early 30s. In the eye of our imagination, we can see the Romany probing the future for his or her clients. He would have used the crystal ball or tarot cards – though some would have employed a method known as palmistry. Reading hands was practised by the ancient Greeks and Napoleon once said 'Faces may tell lies – but never hands!' A fourth form of clairvoyancy is psychometry. In this case the clairvoyant holds a personal item, belonging to the client, a ring or perhaps wrist watch and picks up vibrations – some would say such prediction is a mixed form, combining clairvoyance and telepathy.

Overall the museum does more than preserve Romany culture, any fair-minded person should go out of the door with a better understanding of the Romanies and hopefully a desire to see justice for them. The uncomfortable truth is they continue to be harassed – and the subject of spiteful prejudice.

Tim Le Grice in his thoughtful paper *Gypsies* concludes: *'No less than any other race of people in the world, however widely spread, Romanies must preserve their right to retain a separate culture. The world cannot afford to lose it or them.'*

THE BROOMFIELD HORSE SANCTUARY

AS A MEMBER of the International League for the Protection of Horses, I have a special interest in equine welfare.

With trade barriers coming down in Europe, many of us are deeply concerned about the prospect of British horses, ponies and donkeys being exported live for the dinner table in Europe. The ILPH and the RSPCA have masses of evidence on film of animals suffering on these long unnecessary journeys – and there is further concern about their ultimate fate on the continent. However, a kind of victory was achieved in October 1991 when the British government obtained a temporary exemption and the United Kingdom was able to continue its ban on the export of equines for slaughter.

On the day following that decision in Luxembourg, the International League for the Protection of Horses made the following statement: '*However, we must not lose sight of the fact that this is a temporary reprieve and not a permanent solution. The issue is bound to come up again and EC regulations are going to have to be agreed and implemented at some future date. There is still a great deal of work to be done throughout the EC on stress factors in equine transport. The ILPH will be giving full support to the EC Study Group which is now being set up in Brussels. The ILPH and its allies, such as the Federation Equestre Internationale, will continue to lobby EC member states to persuade them that if there has to be a horse meat trade, then it should be on the hook and not the hoof.*'

It is a curious and sad fact that cruelty to a wide range of animals continues on such an alarming scale in Britain today. The RSPCA, in particular, has sickening evidence.

However, here in West Cornwall we are fortunate to have the Broomfield Horse Sanctuary at Trereife Park and, of course, the horse

LIZ JUPE, the founder and manager of the Broomfield Horse Sanctuary. 'I was restoring antique furniture, and always been around horses all my life. Somebody wanted a second opinion about a pony because they were very worried about its condition. The RSPCA Inspector said "If we had a sanctuary here, I'd take that pony there but the nearest one is too far away as the animal is so weak." That triggered the whole thing, and in January 1986 I started rescuing horses. Broomfield is my paternal grandmother's name … she was a great animal lover.'

Here Liz Jupe is photographed with Vashti, a pure-bred Arab, one of Broomfield's retirement horses, aged twenty-four.

DONKEYS and ponies grazing alongside the Broomfield Sanctuary.

LITTLE BOY BLUE, five years old in 1992, originally bought in very poor condition, from a sale. 'This lady looked after him for a year, and got him really healthy and well, but, due to changed circumstances, offered him to the Sanctuary. We've broken him to ride and to harness.'

has a special place in the hearts and minds of the great majority of British people.

Fellow Bossiney author Ronald Duncan probably said it best when he wrote his moving poem *The Horse* for the Horse of the Year Show:

Where in this wide world can
man find nobility without pride,

friendship without envy or beauty
without vanity? Here, where
grace is laced with muscle, and
strength by gentleness confined.
He serves without servility; he has
fought without enmity. There is
nothing so powerful, nothing less
violent, there is nothing so quick,
nothing more patient.
England's past has been borne on
his back. All our history is his
industry; we are his heirs, he
our inheritance.

The Broomfield Sanctuary was the brave inspired idea of Liz Jupe. Her love of horses is such that Liz and her helpers run the sanctuary with a missionary zeal. It was founded in January 1986 to provide a rescue centre for animals in the Penwith area.

Liz Jupe explains: 'We sometimes take retirement horses too, if they are crippled or ill or if the owner is genuinely unable to continue caring for their horse or pony. We aim to provide food, care, shelter and veterinary treatment for any resident at the Sanctuary. Anyone with a problem with feeding, health or care of their horse or pony may ring our "Horse Help Line". When an animal is mentally and physically recovered, we place them in foster homes so they can lead normal lives. We *never* sell an animal. This also leaves space at the Sanctuary for new residents.'

Fund raising remains Broomfield's biggest challenge. A registered charity, it needs more members and there is an adoption system which may appeal to horse lovers. They also have a special fund to set up a horse hospital, with facilities for x-rays, operations and research, but this is a long-term project. Liz Jupe explains 'Some of the horses or ponies will never be well enough or suitable for foster homes and will have to stay at the Sanctuary. To help with the cost of keeping these animals you can choose one and adopt it for a year. Members are encouraged to pay a minimum of £10 and in return can visit and spend time with the horse or pony and know they are helping him or her and us. If you live some distance away from Broomfield, then we

'EQUINES are essentially herd animals, and here at the Sanctuary we try to establish groups to maintain this interest.' Here is a perfect example: Scrumpy, the Shetland in the foreground, aged four, and Tammy aged fifteen.

will send a photograph and up-to-date report on your adopted animal.

'Our other system is fostering. If you have grazing and space and are interested in helping an animal in need of a good, loving home, then why not foster? Perhaps you need a companion for another horse or pony . . . and some of our foster animals may be suitable for riding too.'

Looking at these horses and ponies at Broomfield – seeing them so well cared for – it is hard to believe that all of them are here because at an earlier stage they were in need of care or attention as a result of sickness, maltreatment, neglect or poor circumstances.

Each one is a triumph for Liz Jupe and her team of helpers.

'LITTLE DORRIT, so-called because she was orphaned at three months and came to Broomfield a month later. Her mother died through swallowing a plastic bag ... a lesson here that plastic litter should not be left in the countryside. Five years old, she was broken to harness in 1991.' ▶

CORNWALL is a curious land – some psychic investigators believe there is a strong connection between ghosts and stone. Moorland granite, used for constructing homes from the earliest times, links us with the past. Can it perhaps absorb the passions and feelings from long-dead people and events and play them back to the sensitives?

JAMAICA INN

JAMAICA Inn deserves inclusion in any Cornish catalogue of curiosities – on at least three counts.

First, there is its haunted reputation. There have been a number of incidents at Jamaica which have defied logical explanation, and I have written about them in *Supernatural Search In Cornwall*, so I will not repeat them here. But this might be the moment to consider the question 'Why are so many spirits associated with inns?' (I don't, of course, mean those that come out of bottles!)

One black night – well past midnight – I stood alone outside Jamaica Inn, sober as any judge – nothing stronger than grapefruit juice and coffee had passed my lips all evening as I had been interviewed there for television by David Young: a programme about ghosts. Now that all the interviewing and filming were over, I wandered around in the darkness and this thought struck. Our inns, over the centuries, have been traditionally convivial places, associated with the business of living – and enjoyment. Furthermore some psychic investigators believe there is a strong connection between ghosts and stone. These investigators believe that, in some strange fashion, the stone can somehow absorb 'emanations' from people, and store them as we might store vision on film or sound on tape. From time to time that 'information' is replayed.

Many of our inns are old buildings, often containing a lot of stonework. I was once talking about ghosts to Alan Nance, the well-known St Austell spiritualist and healer. Alan disliked the term 'ghost' he, though a teetotaller, preferred the word 'spirit'. Anyway Alan believed that, whatever we called 'them', they were characters who were reluctant to leave this, their worldly domain. This may

JAMAICA INN – famous throughout the world. This picture, taken about 40 years ago was kindly lent by Hilda Hambly.

then help to explain why so many of our inns have haunted reputations.

Another curious feature about Jamaica Inn is how it got its name. The name, in fact, dates back to 1789, but the origin remains elusive, although of course, it has always sold *Jamaica* rum. The historian H.L. Douch, though, says there is a strong possibility the location was so unlike Jamaica that somebody thought it worth the cynical comment.

Anyway, thanks to the superlative story-telling of Dame Daphne du Maurier, Jamaica is now one of the most famous inns in Britain. It stands just off the old coach road which ran across the moor to Bodmin.

When Daphne du Maurier first came here in the 1930s Jamaica was a Temperance House, 'hospitable and kindly' were her words. She and her friend Foy Quiller-Couch came on horseback. It was mid-November and during the trip the young girls visited Dozmary Pool and the Cathedral of the Moor at Altarnun, where they met the local vicar. In the evening he came to visit them at Jamaica Inn, and they talked long into the night by the peat fire. Thus the seeds were

Vanishing
Cornwall
Daphne
du Maurier

sown, and *Jamaica Inn*, the novel, began to grow in Daphne's subconscious.

Years later she wrote: '*But if, when you go there, you wonder whether the novel was pure fancy rather than expression of the spirit of the place as I saw it, take a walk behind Jamaica and, one morning before sunrise, climb Rough Tor and listen to the wind and stones. Nothing has really changed since Mary Yellan walked the moors, climbed the tors, and rested in the low dips besides the springs and streams.*

Daphne du Maurier, of course, was more than a gifted novelist. She was a short story writer, biographer and autobiographer, and the visual quality of her writing was so strong that a number of her stories translated naturally into television and cinema films. She had the looks and vitality of an actress and a lovely voice – she was, after all, the daughter of the most distinguished actor manager of his day, Sir Gerald du Maurier. Superficial critics saw her as a romantic novelist, but they were wrong. She was a good psychologist, and her writing diamond sharp, she had brilliant narrative skills and, above all, she was a story teller *par excellence*.

I once asked her about her favourite volume.

'Each book has given me pleasure,' she said, 'but, you know, when it's completed the whole thing fades. Each has its phase.'

She wrote rapidly, usually finishing a book inside twelve months. There were often haunting echoes of the macabre and the supernatural in her tales.

I saw her for the last time at Kilmarth, that lovely residence which inspired her to write *The House on the Strand*. She was then in her 80th year, and kindly autographed some books for me. Incredibly the handwriting had the same strength and flourish as when I first asked for her autograph more than a quarter of a century earlier.

My last memory of her is striding down the drive at Kilmarth with her dogs. Her death at the age of 81 marked the end of a great literary era in Cornwall. She had come to Cornwall in the 1920s and fell in love with the place. It was a love affair that lasted for the rest of her life.

◀ *DAME DAPHNE du Maurier, photographed at Menabilly, the Rashleigh mansion near Par.*

Today at Jamaica Inn, you can visit the Daphne du Maurier room: a room in her honour containing a writing desk and other items from her former home near Par.

It is good that she should be remembered here, for as long as fiction is enjoyed, *Jamaica Inn* will be a favourite.

And, of course, through her writing she was a wonderful ambassador for Cornwall, her books attracting visitors like magnets.

Finally, in a specially constructed building at the Jamaica Inn complex, you can see the work of Walter Potter, the famous Victorian taxidermist. There are more than 10,000 exhibits on display: birds, animals, spiders, butterflies and curios from all over the world, and it is called Mr Potter's Museum of Curiosity.

LADY BROWNING, as she was by her marriage to General Browning, beside her beloved boat. She and her husband, after their wedding at Lanteglos Church, headed in their boat for Frenchman's Creek down on the Helford. She reflected, 45 years on, 'We couldn't have chosen anything more beautiful ...'

SUPERNATURAL CORNWALL

WHETHER WE use the word supernatural or supernormal or paranormal, one fact remains: Cornwall is a vast treasure of strange happenings which defy logical explanation.

However, one thing has changed over the years and changed significantly: the *attitude* of people.

When I first began writing about the supernatural – 'that which is beyond our known laws' – many were inclined to dismiss such events as 'nonsense'. Of course, there are still sceptics but more and more barriers are coming down. This has come about because many men and women of considerable scientific distinction have seriously investigated the supernatural – and continue to do so.

Then there is the evidence. Here in Cornwall alone there have been hundreds of sightings. After more than a quarter of a century of interviewing and investigating I believe the only area for doubt and debate centres on the *nature* of ghosts.

There is a wonderful diversity about Cornwall's 'other population'. In addition to children, men and women in spirit form, we have ghostly cats and dogs, phantom horses and, curiously, a phantom coach and horses only heard – never seen – and only in rough weather at St Just-in-Penwith. There was the guardian spirit of the fishermen of Sennen and there is the spirit of Parson Hawker at Morwenstow. Haunted houses, ancient and modern, there are 'spirits galore' in Kernow.

'What is a ghost?' is the big question.

It's rather like someone from outer space asking 'What is an animal?'

In answer to such a question, we would naturally talk about

THE ROUGH grass, ancient stones and sense of timelessness intertwine with the past and present.

domestic pets like cats and dogs, about livestock such as cattle, sheep and pigs. We would talk about horses who have helped to shape our history, and wildlife mentioning lions, tigers and elephants. Like ghosts, it is a broad question and there is no simple explanation.

The complication deepens too in that some individuals simply refuse to accept the reality of ghosts, dismissing a cast-iron sighting as an illusion: a trick of light or a vivid imagination. If they were to

ACORA, Cornwall's own Romany clairvoyant.

see a patient derive benefit from a spiritual healer, they would mutter 'Mind over matter'. As some folk are colour blind, others are supernatural blind.

The Cornish – the native Cornish, especially the older generation – are very superstitious, and I am wondering if this fact has something to do with the number of ghosts in Cornwall and the amount of healing that goes on. Even people, who say they 'are not superstitious', will frequently 'touch wood', cross fingers, avoid walking under ladders. Times were when magic and superstition exercised a strong influence, over beliefs. Then almost every natural phenomenon had *some* influence over future events – care had to be taken to keep on the right side of the powers behind the birds, the cats, the storms and the stones.

Today, when science seems to be God to so many, it is perhaps no bad thing that old-fashioned superstition lives on in some hearts and minds. Like Christopher Robin, children still avoid cracks in the pavement.

▲ *TINTAGEL – Cornwall's rocky north coast retains an ancient mystery.*

◀ *ST NECTAN'S Glen – perhaps the most haunted place in Cornwall.*

For several years I was the publisher and 'ghost' writer of Acora, the well-known Westcountry Romany clairvoyant. Through contact with both Acora and his wife Jeanette, I have come to put a lot of faith in the old Romany saying: 'Think lucky and you'll be lucky'. I don't think it is wishful thinking either, for highly intelligent students of human behaviour have come to the conclusion that if we *feel* lucky, the odds are that we'll attract good luck.

We seem to have strayed somewhat from ghosts but then that's the supernatural. It's a broad umbrella. It's Cornwall too.

Spiritualists maintain ghosts are the spirits of people who have departed this life – and they may well be right.

Tom Lethbridge, the man they called 'the Einstein of the Paranormal' who lived for some years across the Tamar in Devon, progressed from finding hidden objects through dowsing to exploring the timeless world beyond the thing we call death. Bringing the trained mind of the scientist to the subject, Tom Lethbridge claimed ghosts were 'pictures' produced by human minds. He believed they were 'tape recordings'. He further explored the possibility that there are field forces associated with places like woods and hills – and water. In his splendid book *The Ghost Hunters* Peter Underwood, the President of the Ghost Club, wrote: '*... if this were so, it would explain many previously mysterious appearances, feelings, emotions and experiences. It may well be that the dowser and the ghost hunter should walk hand in hand and this is what Tom Lethbridge frequently did.*'

At this point I am indebted to John Jenkin, a former headmaster at Bodmin, who lives at Golant, hard by Fowey.

Writing to me in February 1992, Mr Jenkin said:

'My maternal uncle, Edwin Chirgwin, Headmaster at St Cleer from 1926 to 1956, was a prolific writer of prose and poetry, in English and Cornish, and was never without paper and pencil to record events and thoughts.

'When he died in 1960 his papers came to me. Among them are 4 or 5 thick books entitled Rustic Jottings. In these he recorded a vast amount of material – anecdotes, folklore, visits to churches, local history, local events etc. Some years ago, I edited them under various headings and have extracted the attached tales from the section Ghosts and Curious Experiences.'

John Jenkin kindly attached the following accounts. They are remarkable in their range and character.

On Ghosts and Curious experiences – written in 1933 at the Vicarage:

'Our vicarage here in St Cleer has the reputation of being haunted by a spider. John Jope the younger son of a vicar of St Cleer was born on March 12 1787 and was curate of St Ive from 1810 to 1814. Later he studied medicine and, suffering from a breakdown in health, went to Portugal, where he died in Lisbon in 1815. His spirit haunted the vicarage and church until his father, Vicar of St Cleer from 1776 to 1844 and a noted ghost-layer, got rid of him by changing his spirit into a spider and giving a crevice in the mantle-pieces as a hiding place. There is a monument to his memory in the church.

'At the Women's Sewing Party at the church today, the Vicar's wife related a curious experience which she had yesterday, and my wife, who was in the conversation, has passed the details to me.

'She had gone out and on her return found that the servants had left before 3pm whereas their time for going was 5pm. Evening came and she and the Vicar were reading when three taps were heard, as though struck on a brass plate. There is no brass plate beneath the door knocker. The Vicar answered the knocks but when he opened the door there was nobody there and nobody spoke. He suggested that the person who was apparently hiding should reveal himself but there was no response and he returned to the fireside. While he was at the door his wife heard two further knocks of which he was unaware.

'Later it transpired that the Vicar's mother had suddenly become ill to the point of death and while word was on the way from Worcester she repeatedly asked for her daughter. The servants explained their absence by stating that they had fled in panic because of the sounds they had endured during the afternoon and which they could neither trace nor account for.

'My friend, a local architect, told me his father was hoeing potatoes one afternoon when he suddenly turned around and exclaimed, "Hullo, Alf Pearce". Now, Alf Pearce was his brother-in-law and had apparently looked over the hedge. Calling himself a fool he went on with his work because he knew that Alf Pearce was many miles away. Next day they got word that Mr Pearce had been accidentally killed on the previous day at the very moment that he had apparently appeared.

'My neighbour, Miss Roberts, told me that her father died in London. Miss Roberts was the child of his first wife and always lived with grand-parents in St Cleer. One evening she was sitting by the fire with her grandmother when suddenly someone stepped on her foot. She took little notice except to marvel at the speed with which her grandmother must have brought her foot back.

'A few moments later the act was repeated and she asked why her foot was being stepped on. She was not altogether surprised when her grandmother denied having done such a thing because the old lady was entirely lost in the book she was reading and it was evident she had not moved.

'The next letter from London brought news that Miss Roberts's father had died at the time her foot was stepped on. It must be said that no one was further from her thoughts at that moment because she had always lived with her grandparents and rarely saw her father and his second family'.

Written in 1932 – King Doniert:

'At a Whist Drive in St Agatha's Room last night, Parson Lewis told me that a villager had been awakened during the previous night by a vision of King Doniert, who had said to him, "You are my namesake, tell them to leave me alone".

'The man, whose name is King, woke his wife and described the vision as a tall, elderly man with a white beard, wearing a crown and a white robe, with the hair curled upward at the neck.

'This week, King Doniert's tomb, about 800 yards from the parish church, has been excavated, the operations being carried out by the Liskeard Old Cornwall Society and the Office or Works. There is now much speculation in the parish as to whether those who have carried out the work will have the same fate as that supposedly suffered by those who excavated Tutankhamun's tomb a few years ago.'

(Telepathy, communication between one mind and another without the use of speech, is clearly confirmed in some of these accounts; and, of course, if anybody did suffer as a result of the King Doniert excavations, I should be very interested to know. MW)

Frederick William Densham was one of the oddest of our Cornish clerics – some would say *the* oddest – and even today Warleggan, his old Bodmin Moor parish, has an isolated air, an impression intensified by the remote farms of slate and granite.

WARLEGGAN, Densham's moorland parish church.

He died alone in his rectory in 1953, surrounded by barbed wire and a high fence.

Roger Farnworth has renamed the Rectory. Today it is the Rookery. Roger Farnworth told me how a family holidaying at The Rookery cut short their holiday and, as a result, he offered them a replacement holiday at a reduced rate.

Peter Hames, his wife and son, who had arrived on a Saturday, declined the offer, and this extract from his letter to Roger Farnworth explains why they did not come back to the old Rectory.

Dear Mr Farnworth,

'. . . *the following night (Sunday) we went to bed around midnight and I fell asleep almost immediately, the next thing I knew was that my wife woke me around 1 am in a very distressed state. It took me some time to calm her down sufficiently to explain to me what happened. She contends that she was sitting up in bed when the room went cold, a figure appeared in the area of the doorway onto the landing. It moved across the room towards her and disappeared through the wall, between her bed and the window, after having brushed past her, leaving her with a cold tingling sensation. She describes the figure as an old man with wispy grey hair and a long grey beard, dressed in an emerald green cloak. Throughout all this time the landing light was on, it had been left on for my son in case he awoke during the night.*

'My wife was not able to go back to sleep that night and I sat up with her until around 4.30am when it became light. We then both slept for around three to four hours. We had decided during that night to leave the following morning, however, with the light of day my wife decided to try another night. The following night again she could not settle and thus the next morning we decided the only thing to do was to move on, which we did and completed our holiday by taking bed and breakfast in Tintagel. I did not explain all this in my letter to you when we left as we both felt rather foolish, as neither myself nor my wife had experienced anything like this previously.

'When we came to Warleggan we had only read your brochure, on the Sunday we read the short passage in the Vanishing Cornwall *book by Daphne du Maurier. It is only since leaving that we have read the various references to the Reverend Densham in the books by Michael Williams, particularly the manuscript prepared by your late wife and produced in* Cornish Mysteries.

'This persuaded us that perhaps my wife has seen something and that I should write and explain in detail. Yours sincerely, Peter Hames.'

For our next supernatural destination we travel to Tintagel. The parish of Tintagel and surrounding coastline and countryside have triggered a remarkable amount of paranormal activity. Sonia and I lived at Bossiney for ten years and in the cottage attached to the hotel we heard phantom footsteps on the staircase on numerous occasions. It was at Bossiney Mound that I had my first major supernatural experience on Midsummer Eve 1965. I have also interviewed more than twenty people who have had experiences in the area which defied all logical explanation.

Why Tintagel and district?

It could, of course, be a combination of factors.

First, having lived there for a decade, and being known as an investigator into the supernatural, people may have come forward more readily, more easily. But the answer is certainly deeper.

Maybe that controversial Anglican priest Bernard Walke got to the heart of the matter when he said: *'I do not know what historical evidence there is for connecting Tintagel with the Holy Grail legend, but I am convinced something of spiritual import happened here . . .'*

Perhaps the perceptive Arthur Mee, editor of *The King's England*, touched a key point; back in the 1930s he wrote: *'In the evening when the sun is sinking into the Atlantic from something like a flaming battlefield we can think it is true about Arthur and his knights. A deep sense of something mysterious comes upon us . . .'*

There is undoubtedly a strong atmosphere at Tintagel. Moreover the area is strong in genuine history and legend, all of which helps to fan our imagination. The human brain often prepares us, but it would be wrong to explain it all away as 'imagination'.

In the past decade I have interviewed members of a psycho-expansion group here in the south-west, all seemingly responsible people, many of them doing worthwhile work in the community. They claim not only to have lived in Arthurian times but to have been Arthurian characters. One housewife, who lives and works just across the River Tamar in Devon, is convinced she was Arthur in earlier life. I have met 'Arthur' on more than twenty occasions, several times interviewing 'him' on specific Arthurian matters.

Psycho-expansion is a technique which enables the individual to explore and develop his or her sense of awareness. The claim is the mind is therefore able to move in time and space. It is time travel.

I have written about 'Arthur' at length in *Somerset Mysteries* when Polly Lloyd of Bristol was co-author. Here is what I wrote about the actual interviewing process:

'During these interviews I have been impressed by the variety of changes in her personality. In regression for example, she sits differently; her voice becomes noticeably lower in key. Listening to this Aquarian lady you are aware that she is giving a kind of commentary, but no matter-of-fact commentary, no plateau of emotion. At times she is genuinely troubled, and other times highly amused. You, the interviewer, are forced to one of two conclusions: she is either a very talented actress (as far as I know she has never been on the stage) or you are watching and listening to something not quite of this

LYNETTE KNIGHT, behind the wheel of her car, once more travels the road where she encountered a ghostly figure.

world.'

For the purposes of this chapter in *Curious Cornwall*, one fact needs underlining. In all the interviews 'Arthur' emphasised that Tintagel did, in fact, feature in the life and times of the *Once and Future King.*

The cynic, of course, will snort, but those who believe in reincarnation and psycho-expansion will accept this as evidence.

Anyway my visit to Tintagel in March 1992 had nothing to do with King Arthur.

Lynette Knight, a Taurus subject and member of a well-known Tintagel family, told me: 'I was driving from Camelford to my home in Tintagel cemetery when I saw a light in the hedge, like a torch. "Who's that walking on the road at this time of night?" I thought. As I got closer the light vanished from the left hand side of the road, the cemetery side; by now I'd slowed down to about 15 miles an hour, and I could clearly see this figure crossing the road ahead, carrying a lantern. He was wearing a long black hooded cloak, like a monk. Then he swung around, darted in front of the car to the cemetery side of the road again, and disappeared into the hedge. I could see the figure very clearly, but both times it was a side view so I didn't see his face, but the figure was certainly solid – nothing vague or misty.

'I can see him – or it – now. No question of imagination. It was all so clear. I wasn't frightened at the time, but mum and dad would confirm I was in quite a state when I got back home a few minutes later. The odd thing is somebody else saw the figure in the same place about ten years earlier.'

In a separate conversation with Lynette's mother, she told me: 'Lynette was in a terrible state when she arrived back home. I said to her, "Anybody would think you've seen a ghost," and Lynette replied "I think I have!"

So another ghostly monk sighting for Tintagel, and possibly an anniversary ghost. Clearly Tintagel's 'other population' is reluctant to leave.

CREATIVITY OF CORNWALL

THERE ARE minds within minds, and I believe curiosity and creativity are close relations.

Creativity, more than any other attribute, distinguishes men and women from the animal kingdom – and computers. Without creativity, we would still be living in caves. The moment of insight, that sudden flash from the unconscious, is the main facet of creative work. It resembles the flash of understanding that makes a joke funny. A sudden laugh is a kind of minor creativity.

Creativity remains one of the most mysterious of all psychological phenomena.

Dame Barbara Cartland, who produces a novel a week, says she goes into a trance and lets her unconscious do the work. Robert Louis Stevenson dreamed many of his stories, particularly when he was hard up and needed a story to sell.

Elias Howe spent five years failing to perfect his sewing machine. Then, one night, he dreamt of being captured by savages who dragged him before their king. The king gave him an ultimatum: produce the sewing machine within 24 hours or die by the spear. Howe failed to meet the deadline, and saw his executioners appear. But, as the spears rose to pierce him, his terrible fears fled. In a flash, he saw the spearheads had eye-shaped holes in their tips. Awakening with the sudden insight that the eye of the sewing machine needle should be near its point, Howe dressed and dashed to his workshop to make his model. We should remember him – and his dream – every time we go to buy a suit.

There is great creativity here in Cornwall. Painters and potters, sculptors and writers have been fired by the spirit of ancient Kernow.

Native genius has flowered in the invention of Humphrey Davy and Richard Trevithick.

Much has been written and created here – probably more than anywhere outside London.

Why?

The question is fascinating, almost inevitable. But the answer is curiously elusive. Back in the 1960s I was doing a lot of magazine and newspaper work on the arts in Cornwall, and during interviews with distinguished painters the question often came to the surface.

Sometimes an interview grew into a friendship, my meeting with Charles Simpson being one such case. Charles was a member of the old school of painters – he had known people like Stanhope Forbes, Sir Alfred Munnings and 'Lamorna' Birch. He was also a very fine descriptive writer, but had little time for the then 'modern' trends in painting.

Here are some notes from our very first meeting – appearing in book form for the first time – reading them 30 years on, for me, is a curious experience: a different person who happens to share your name.

MW: Cornwall has attracted many painters. What do you think draws them to the place?

CS: One of the great attractions is the climate, the light, the brilliant sunshine. Another great attraction was the wildlife of Cornwall: the great number of birds and butterflies.

MW: Apart from the obvious advantages of Cornwall – the brilliant light, the colours, the availability of studios and the comparatively cheap cost of living – do you think there is another more subtle factor? You can call it atmosphere or a magical quality – something that stirs the creative spirit.

CS: There is an atmosphere of age in Cornwall. The early history of man still seems to brood over the Cornish moors and hills. I have always taken much interest in the remains of such places as Chysauster . . . one really felt one was looking at one of early man's homes. Here in Cornwall I've found many landscapes and marine subjects which were finer than anywhere else I've painted. I've painted in rocky coves and on sandy beaches with seagulls and cormorants overhead. At Hayle Estuary I did some of my best work of the open water with flights of wild duck, gannets, puffins, lapwings and numerous other wild birds. One of the first of these paintings won a silver medal at the Paris Salon.

MW: What kind of colony did you have at Newlyn in those early days?

CS: A very happy society. Stanhope Forbes was the presiding genius; he gave many parties and concerts at his house, he himself played the cello. He was really the man who made Newlyn.

I was lucky to meet Charles Simpson while still in my twenties. Despite a generation gap, he was a considerable influence. Thanks to Charles, I found myself walking across places like Hannibal's Carn – a new world for me – now I began to understand the shade and the subtlety of the Penwith landscape.

Writers too have been drawn to Cornwall. Another interviewee, at about the same time, who became a friend, was Wallace Nichols living at Usticke Haven, a house on the outskirts of Penzance, dating from Elizabethan times, standing behind Nancealverne, the former home of Judge J.W. Scobell Armstrong.

An hour in the company of Wallace Nichols was never dull or wasted. He was full of anecdotes. He had met Churchill and Elgar; Dylan Thomas and Lawrence of Arabia. He could and should have written a brilliant autobiography. He spoke five modern languages and several obscure ones, including Egyptian and Babylonian. In conversation he coped with an impediment yet when he read you a piece of poetry the hesitations vanished. Clarity and confidence growing ultimately taking over, his voice suddenly, surprisingly deepening, he would reveal the beauty and the meaning of every line.

Wallace was a talented all-rounder: poet, historical novelist, detective short story writer, boys' adventure book author and essayist, he produced more than sixty books.

As Charles Simpson helped me to *see* things, Wallace Nichols helped me in writing. He knew I had ambitions as a publisher, and I am only sorry he never lived to see the creation of Bossiney.

In our first interview I asked him about Cornwall's influence.

'Cornwall's aura of the past,' he said, 'certainly stimulates the writer's imagination. If you go through Madron village towards the open moors beyond, you are on the edge of prehistoric country, filled with the memories and memorials of a lost race . . . one feels near the

WALLACE NICHOLS, the writer, who lived on the outskirts of Penzance.

beginnings of things on a Cornish moor. For my part, the triangle formed by lines drawn from Madron to Morvah thence to Zennor and back to Madron, is the most wildly magical area of West Cornwall and I would willingly surrender any of the coves and beaches for its astringent beauty. The atmosphere of Cornwall has helped my imagination . . . even when not writing about the county. But really the writer – he should be able to write anywhere.'

In search of the answer – or answers – to the question of Cornwall's magnetism, I have moved forward thirty years. In April 1992; a conversation with Ken Duxbury, the author and painter who lives at St. Breward high on Bodmin Moor. His watercolours not only capture the shade and shape of the moor but the very spirit of the place. It is a curious fact Bodmin Moor has attracted relatively few painters.

Anyway, here is Ken Duxbury in his moorland cottage talking about this elusive subject:

'Well, artists – no matter in what field they work – are essentially creative people. They wouldn't be artists otherwise, and creativity responds to inspiration. Cornwall inspires.

'Why? I've asked myself that question many times. The nearest I've come to a solution that makes any sense is that here in Cornwall one lives in closer contact with one's roots. Closer to elemental things than one may do in the Home Counties or the Midlands. There is a quality about the place, and you'll find it too in the Highlands of Scotland, in the Lake District and Wales, but here in Cornwall we have the added bonus of an incomparable coastline surrounding almost the entire land. It is something to do with the quality of the air and the light. After all, we are the first to get that air after it has made an oceanic crossing of thousands of miles, so it's crystal clear and unpolluted.

'It may sound fanciful, Michael, but, you know, polluted environs tend to breed polluted souls. I suppose by that I really mean souls without much character. Uninspired. Here there is true character in the land and in the people. It may be a little abrasive at times and astringent. But it's elemental and rings true . . . and that's what draws truly creative people to Cornwall.

'As for the moor – Bodmin Moor I'm talking about – you said just now you were puzzled that so few artists painted here. Well maybe the moor doesn't inspire others, but it certainly inspires me and I

PETER LANYON, the Cornish painter with an international reputation, at his home just outside St Ives.

paint it endlessly. Like the ocean it's never the same in colour or feeling from one moment to another. If you are correct – and I'm not sure that you are – maybe the fact that we have the more extensive Dartmoor alongside, so to speak, bleeds them off to Devon for their subjects. Most likely it is because they do not actually live here on the moor, so never discover its unique magic.

'But make no mistake, that's why creative people are drawn to Cornwall. They can scent the magic!'

In any analysis of creativity in Cornwall, we must not forget the significant contribution made by native painters. In the 18th century there was the portrait painter John Opie, a contemporary of Devon's Sir Joshua Reynolds, who went on to become Professor of Painting at the Royal Academy. Horace Walpole said of him: 'There is a new genius . . . a Cornish lad of nineteen who has taught himself to colour in a bold masterly style.'

Then in this century we had the gifted Peter Lanyon who died tragically early at the age of 46 in a gliding accident over Somerset. He intensely disliked the term 'modern art', loathing labels and watertight compartments. 'Art is continuous', he once told me, 'the artist is constantly changing people's vision. I've been called a lot of things in my time, but I see myself in the tradition of Constable, Turner, Nash and Cotman. The language I use is strange and is therefore called abstract.'

Happily, today, native Cornish art flourishes in various parts of Kernow. Margo Maeckelberghe of Penzance is a regular exhibitor at Newlyn and St Ives, and has exhibited in London and overseas. She is a landscape painter and Cornwall is the subject of much of her work but by no means all. Peter Lanigan-O'Keefe, writing in her London catalogue of 1990, said '. . . *Cornwall is a land of strange contrasts; it is a Celtic land, full of timeless quality, something quite indefinable but something which Margo explores in her paintings in such a way as to let us in a little on the secret . . .*'

Jack Pender, a Mousehole man, has spent a lifetime – well, almost a lifetime – looking 'out on two granite quays enclosing a small harbour with a wide vista of sea and sky beyond.. I'm constantly aware of the interplay of space and solid, shape and colour, and of the relationship of boat to boat, to quay, to sea and to man.'

On the other coast at St Ives, Bryan Pearce has been called 'the Miracle Painter', a reference to his suffering from a rare genetic disorder. St Ives is the window of his world, and Mr H.S. Ede, who was at the Tate, said 'If anyone is in need of peace, trust and joy, they will find it in the work of Bryan Pearce.'

CHERRY BLOSSOM by Mary Martin

Upalong in the Tamar Valley is Mary Martin, another fine Cornish painter. Almost all Mary's work is done out of doors. She works swiftly, capturing the changing light of the valley, and the river. You might find her painting in a field of daffodils, or piece of woodland, in an orchard or sloping landscape blazing with colour and vitality.

There are, of course, other Cornish painters, but these four natives, in their differing ways, underline the diversity and the creativity of Cornwall.

A CURIOUS rock formation on Bodmin moor. Ken Duxbury, who lives not far away, holds interesting theories about the influence of the moor on the artist. ►

THE DUKE of Cornwall – a good judge of horses as can be seen in this picture – and no less a judge of modern buildings. But his Duchy can show architecture of many kinds, much qualifying for the adjective 'curious'.

CURIOUS BUILDINGS

OUR DUKE of Cornwall has some strong views on architecture – and rightly so.

On his visits to Cornwall the Duke must be intrigued by the curious character of some of our Cornish architecture, especially some of the older buildings. Like ghosts we have more than our fair share.

I never come through St Columb Major without thinking of William White, an architect who was born in 1825 and died in 1900. White may not have been an eccentric but he left a distinct legacy in this part of Cornwall. The sad thing is, the vast majority of holidaymakers now hurry past the town, speeding along the fast and sometimes dangerous by-pass. Arthur Mee referred to it as 'the sleeping-place of the Cornwall Arundells (one of our great Cornish families) brought here from their great house of Lanherne for their last rest.' St Columb is a stronghold of the ancient sport of Cornish hurling, and Jack Crapp, the Gloucestershire and England cricketer, was born here.

But getting back to William White: no traveller interested in Cornish architecture can ignore him or his work – working as he did on something like twenty major sites. Some of his most distinctive works remain in and around the town. Thanks to William White, St Columb Major has a special place in Westcountry architecture.

His first St Columb client was one Dr Samuel Edmund Walker who wanted the old Rectory rebuilt, not only for himself, the incumbent, but as a possible Bishop's Palace. Around the middle of the last century, politics in the Cornish Church were largely angled on the location of the Cathedral; with Bodmin and Truro rivals for that accolade, St Columb was suggested as a third alternative – but it was not

THE OLD RECTORY, St Columb.

to be.

Nevertheless White's St Columb Rectory with its moat is undoubtedly one of the most picturesque in the whole diocese. Later it became a hotel and country club. Standing today in its two acres of gardens, it is interesting to reflect how the whole fate of St Columb would have been different had the Cathedral been built here – and the Bishop's Palace had become a reality. Much of the prosperity, which today belongs to Truro, would have come naturally to the town. Such is history – and the result of political choice.

William White, who was born in Northampton but began his career in Truro, was something of a revolutionary in his Victorian heyday: an architect capable of producing modern progressive designs. His bank, built in 1857, is another notable St Columb landmark; later used by the Ministry of Labour, it is now a solicitor's office. With brown and multi-coloured stones and coloured bands of red brick, it's rated one of the finest Victorian Gothic buildings west of the Tamar.

Other White legacies in the area are Penmellyn, a delightful slate house on the northern shoulder of the town, and Trewan Hall, a splendid sixteenth-century manor which he restored.

All four remain today: living reminders of William White's vision and vitality: no ordinary creator, a man who once said: 'Style as such must be thrown to winds . . .' – and who meant it.

Now we go north: to the Cornwall-Devon border – well, almost – to Launceston Castle.

I first met Launceston Castle in the eye of imagination: thanks to the superlative story-telling of Daphne du Maurier. This is where Sir Richard Grenville was imprisoned in *The King's General*: a prisoner of his own side. Towering over the roofs of the town, it was known as 'Castle Terrible'. The Normans chose this location wisely, for the castle provided a good vantage point from which mile upon mile of landscape between Bodmin Moor and the wilderness of Dartmoor could be watched and strategically controlled. *The King's General* remains my favourite Cornish novel; it is astonishing to reflect the

WHITE'S BANK at St Columb.

TWO VIEWS of the imposing Trewan Hall.

story has never been translated for the television or cinema screen.

I first saw the castle physically in the 1950s when I brought a cricket touring team to Launceston for the last match of a week-long tour. We played Launceston Cricket Club on the Launceston College ground, and won in the very last over of the evening – one of the best games of cricket in which I had the luck to be captain – we celebrated after the match with drinks and sandwiches in the White Hart. In those days not a single cricket club in Cornwall had a bar!

A few years later I paid my first visit to the Castle, and again I was lucky in that Charles Causley – now Dr Causley – took me on a personally conducted tour. I had come to the town to interview him for a magazine article, and he suggested we work up an appetite before lunching at the White Hart by touring the castle ruins; with his remarkable local knowledge he brought it all to life.

Charles Causley is one of our greatest native writers – many of us felt he should have succeeded John Betjeman as Poet Laureate. In September 1984 *The Western Morning News* devoted a leader to 'The Case for Causley'. The last two paragraphs read:

'The experience of a poet is our own experience but sharper and clearer than we can coin it. Causley has spent most of his life as a schoolmaster in Launceston. People who suggest that this may have been limiting miss the point. The poems about children (Maloney, or the splendid, immortal Timothy Winters) are no more "local" than those about the Cornish sculptor Nevil Northey Burnard, or about Keats and Teignmouth: the ballad of Charlotte Dymond may be set on Bodmin Moor, but it is really placeless. Causley pointed out, years ago, that the man who comes home from travel boasting of strange experiences and new sights meets, always, the same response from the poet: "You smiled, for you had seen it all before." His most recent poems only underline the fact that an idea may be born as readily in Australia or Canada as in Mevagissey or at Bayeux or on the road to Marazion.

'Asked to list Charles Causley's qualities, one would have to include technical ability (his technique can be dazzling), humour, narrative talent (his ballads are as readable as Jeffrey Archer, and considerably more imaginative), artfulness as well as art. His humanity illuminates every line he writes. And above all, his poetry is available. Any newspaper reader can read a Causley poem and "get it".

LAUNCESTON CASTLE, one of the truly great landmarks the traveller sees as he approaches Cornwall from across the Tamar.

But not all of it. His poems can be read again and again. On the twentieth reading they still seem unforced, natural as the leaves to the tree, as "conversational" as a letter to a friend. But at each reading a new felicity, a new insight, is revealed. His work is indeed both popular and good. There is no better recommendation for the Laureateship.'

But getting back specifically to Launceston Castle, does it really deserve a place in this Cornish catalogue of curiosity?

It does.

Back in 1981 I commissioned Joan Rendell, a well-known Launceston lady and Cornish Bard, to write *Gateway to Cornwall*. It's now been out of print for several years, but there is a splendid reference to the Castle:

'Dramatic as it is to see Launceston for the first time when travelling from

LAUNCESTON CASTLE sits solidly above the town as residents go about their lives, apparently oblivious to its presence the other side of the wall.

the east on the old A30 road or the new by-pass which has taken over the former road's mantle, perhaps the most surprising, and even alarming, view is when approaching from the north, after passing through St Stephens. At that point a splendid view of the castle and the town climbing up the slopes beneath awaits the traveller but – surprise, surprise, the castle keep is leaning. It looks as though it might even slip over to one side, right on to the town beneath it. Many are the visitors who, seeing the castle from that viewpoint for the first time, have rubbed their eyes and wondered if they have been driving for too long or if perhaps they shouldn't have had that glass of wine at lunch or dinner. No, it is not an optical illusion, the castle keep really does lean, three feet two inches out of alignment, to be exact. What is more it has been leaning a bit more with each year that has passed, because when it was surveyed in 1903 the keep was only two feet nine inches out of alignment. But it is unlikely to slide any further; after it was surveyed in 1966 Department of the Environment building experts carried out magical and completely undetectable work to ensure that the keep remained stable probably for all time. They couldn't put it back on an even keel but they certainly did the next best thing and now Launceston Castle has an added curiosity value.'

Just a final point before we leave this grand old Cornish town. The pronunciation is LANSON.

One of my favourite Cornish buildings is the Old Village Post Office in the Tintagel main street. Now a National Trust property, it is a rare survival of a 14th century domestic dwelling. Especially eye-catching is its wildly uneven roof, like a storm-ridden sea, and as I write in spring 1992 comes the news that this ancient roof structure has deteriorated to such an extent a complete re-roofing is necessary. It is heartening to know great care will be taken to ensure the new roof will follow the precise contours of the old. So, arguably the most photographed roof in Cornwall will continue to attract men and women with their cameras.

Tintagel is the name on the map, but times were when the village was called Trevena and Tintagel referred to the parish with its baker's dozen of hamlets.

During the early part of the last century all post was brought from Camelford by foot messenger, but in 1844 the Post Office created a letter-receiving office at Trevena, hiring a room here for that purpose which flourished until 1892. Three years later the property was auctioned and knocked down to a group of artists who found the cost of preservation beyond their means and in 1900 the Trust purchased the building for a nominal £100. Surely the National Trust never spent a better £100.

I first came to know the Old Village Post Office in the mid-1960s, when Harry Cann was the custodian. Harry was a sporting hero of mine. I was not old enough to see him keep goal for Plymouth Argyle as a professional, but my grandfather Edgar Williams, a very fine footballer in his day, and later a firm but fair referee, who went on to become a Vice-President of the Cornwall County Football Association, told me Harry was a very accomplished goal-keeper. I did though see Harry in the sunset of his career, playing in the South Western League, when he still showed great skill and anticipation, especially in cutting off centres from the wingers. So any visit to the Old Village Post Office had the delightful bonus of Harry Cann recalling his professional days at Home Park. He was a fund of footballing stories.

One of his favourites concerned an elderly England selector, who back in the 1930s, came down to Plymouth to watch a young footballer for possible representative selection. England selectors were inclined to dress rather formally in those days, and as the team were about to come on to the field, an old Plymouth Argyle player, with something of an anti-Establishment reputation, passing the England selector, lifted the gentleman's hat from his head with the words 'Good afternoon, you baldheaded old bugger!' The unfortunate young footballer, though entirely innocent, never won promotion.

THE OLD Post Office at Tintagel.

CURIOSITIES OF CORNISH SPORT

FOR JUST two days out of the calendar, St Columb changes its character and mood.

On Shrove Tuesday and the second Saturday in Lent, it has the air of a town under siege. Windows barricaded and cars tucked away: a hint of Civil War hangs over the slate roofs and narrow streets, and, in a way, it *is* Civil War. These are the days when Town and Country do battle.

Hurling's origin lies deep in Cornwall's past, as vague and hazy as the landscape on a misty morning. Some believe it stems from the Bronze Age. Once it was a popular sport but the negative Puritans condemned it and today, St Columb is the last real stronghold. A circle of ancient stones, standing at St Cleer, is known as The Hurlers. Legend has it that some young Cornishmen rashly played on a Sunday and, as a punishment, they were turned to stone.

In 1823, a boy, William Webb Ellis by name, picked up the ball and broke the law by running with it on the turf of Rugby School, thereby creating the modern game of Rugby Football. Here in cornwall we feel justified in claiming that our Hurlers were the real pioneers. An account of the sport by Richard Carew in 1602 uncannily anticipates some of Rugby's laws and patterns by more than two centuries.

Hurling differs from Rugby and soccer in that the object is to take the ball back to one's own goal or alternatively to carry it over the parish boundary. The goals, two stone troughs, are a mile outside the town: one at Cross Putty, the other at Tregamere Turning on the Wadebridge road. The ball itself, about the size of the cricketer's, is made of light wood and encased with silver, bearing the inscription:

THE ANCIENT sport of Hurling at St Columb Major – an energetic leap to capture the silver ball outside the Red Lion.

'Town and Country, do your best, For in this parish I must rest.'

Like wrestling, Hurling was tougher in times past. In the days of the first Elizabeth a match sometimes lasted two or three days. One chronicler recalled men 'returning home as from pitched batialle, with bloody pates, bones broken and out of joint, and such bruises as serve to shorten their days.'

Here in Cornwall Rugby is almost a religion or way of life. The link with Hurling is obvious. It is an odd fact that whereas Cornish Rugby has produced as many as 30 England internationals – admittedly not all of them natives – only two Cornishmen have played test cricket for England, and only one has worn the international shirt at soccer. These figures, of course, tell their own story.

For all the passion and galaxy of individual talent, our Cornish team has only won the county championship on two occasions – against Durham at Redruth as long ago as 1908 and against Yorkshire at Twickenham in 1991.

I had the luck to be at Twickenham. Before a capacity gate of 57,000 – the great majority Cornish people from Cornwall or living in exile in England – Cornwall staged a remarkable comeback. Seemingly out of the game at one point, we stormed back to sensational victory in extra time, winning by 29 points to 20. Yorkshire,

CORNWALL AT the line out.

from a position of apparent victory, were buried. At the hour, the championship seemed destined for Yorkshire – a 13 point lead – at which stage a Cornish parson in the west stand said 'Now we need

CORNWALL doing battle against Devon on Cornish soil.

to pray'. By some miracle, the Cornish giant stirred from his slumber. suddenly it were as if Hellfire Corner had come to London. In the last 15 minutes of the game and in the first 12 minutes of extra time, Cornwall scored 26 points without a Yorkshire reply! The black and gold hordes sang, the black and white flags of St Piran were waved as they have never been waved before – raw emotion carried our sixteen Cornish heroes on to history. There were sixteen Cornish players because captain Chris Alcock, midway through the second half, had to leave the field with an ankle injury.

It was a day we Cornish will never forget.

And the last word must surely be from farmer and prop forward John May: 'Now I believe in reincarnation'.

Another curious facet of our sporting scene is Cornish wrestling – or 'wrastling' as the proper Cornish say.

Nobody is sure of its genesis but historians tell us that at the Battle of Agincourt, where banners depicted the different county contingents, the Cornishmen had two wrestlers on theirs. Richard

Trevithick, who invented a high-pressure steam engine by the age of 25, was in his spare time an excellent wrestler, but Polkinghorne (sometimes spelt without the e) stands at the top of the tree, as one of the best half-dozen Cornishmen the sport has produced.

Present-day Cornish wrestling is a robust business. But in

Polkinghorne's time it was positively brutal, especially when the Devonshire style was employed. The Devonians, wearing boots soaked in bullocks' blood and hardened at the fire, hacked away at the shins of their Cornish opponents who, as a protective measure, wrapped their legs below the knee in skillibegs or bands of hay.

There is a tablet on the roadside wall of the Red Lion commemorating Polkinghorne's great match against Abraham Cann, Champion of Devon, for the West of England Crown: £200 a side; the best of three falls. It took place on Tamar Green at Devonport on Monday, October 23, 1826, 17,000 spectators turned up and bets of £100 were wagered. Cann, who was three stone lighter, wore a pair of shoes, the toes of which had been baked into flints! Polkinghorne, though, struck first. Lifting Cann from the ground, he threw him over his shoulder and planted him on his back. Jubilant Cornish supporters leapt into the ring and embraced their champion, but in the ensuing rounds both men 'played for wind'. Then Cann began to kick furiously, upsetting the Cornishman's balance and throwing him on his back – the first that the four stickers (umpires or referees, two from Devon and two from Cornwall) allowed him.

In his book *Cornish Characters & Strange Events*, Sabine Baring-Gould vividly described the closing stages: *'Disputes now disturbed the umpires, and their number was reduced to two. In the eighth round Polkinghorne's strength began to fail, and a dispute was improvised which occasioned another hour's delay. With wind regained and strength revived the tenth round was contested with absolute fury and, taking kicking with fine contempt, Polkinghorne gripped Cann with leonine majesty, lifted him from the earth in his arms, turned him over his head and dashed him to the ground with stunning force.*

'As the Cornishman dropped on his knee the fall was disputed, and turn was disallowed. Polkinghorne then left the ring amid a mighty clamour, and by reason of his default the stakes were awarded to Cann.'

After the match, Cann wrote to the Cornishman promising: *'I will take off my boots and play bare legged with you and you may have two of the hardest and heaviest shoes you like that can be made of leather in the County of Cornwall. And you shall be allowed to stuff yourself as high as the armpits to any extent not exceeding the size of a Cornish pack of wool. And I will further engage not to kick you if you don't kick me.'*

Seemingly though Polkinghorne did not believe the promise

CORNISH WRESTLING.

because no return match took place. And who can blame him? Anyway, the epic match with Cann achieved a kind of immortality in that, the deeds were turned into a ballad and sung to the tune *The Night I Married Susy.*

James Polkinghorne lived until 1854, 28 years after the battle of Tamar Green, and as long as Cornishmen 'wrastle' his name will be remembered.

Happily the sport lives on today and if you have the luck to be in Cornwall when a wrestling match is scheduled, make the most of the chance. Particularly if the Cornishmen are tackling the Bretons, for on such an occasion you will catch a truly Celtic flavour. The ritual before Cornu-Breton Inter-Celtic Championships can be impressive, with the Wrestlers' Oath being spoken in four languages: English and Cornish, French and Breton.

A CURIOUS POSTSCRIPT

IN CORNWALL curious facts and facets are scattered all over the place.

As I come towards the end of this journey across *Curious Cornwall*, I have decided to try and give some indication of the range of curiosity in terms of subject and geography.

Penzance is no bad place from which to start such an excursion: the first and last town in Cornwall or the last and first – or would St Just dispute either claim?

Either way, let us call at the Union Hotel in historic Chapel Street. In these days of immediate communication, when the press of a switch on our television set can bring us news from the other side of the globe or the moon, it is hard to us to appreciate the times when news spread only as fast as the method of transport – on foot or horse or by boat or ship.

When we come to the Union Hotel we are reminded of this basic truth.

Here are the facts which give the hotel its special place in the field of historic communications.

On the 21st day of October 1805, Admiral Lord Nelson took on the French Fleet at Trafalgar, off Cadiz, Spain. It was a windless sea, and a bitter encounter for both sides. The French lost eighteen vessels that autumn day – which was virtually the end of Napoleon's navy as a striking force. But we British also suffered. Just after the victory was reported to Horatio Nelson, he died of his wounds – hit by a sniper's bullet.

The British fleet, making for home and heading for Plymouth, ran into bad weather and put into Mount's Bay. An officer from the

BOSSINEY AUTHOR Sarah Foot at the Union Hotel, Penzance, looking at the balcony from which the news of Nelson's death was announced.

schooner *Pickle* came ashore and hurried up Chapel Street to the Union Hotel where a banquet, attended by the Mayor of Penzance, was in progress and from the balcony of the dining room, now called the Trafalgar Room, the news was announced.

I wonder how many Penzance residents know of another link between the town and the Napoleonic days. Lemon Hart was a Jewish merchant of Penzance who had the monopoly of victualling rum to the Royal Navy throughout the Napoleonic Wars. He lies buried in the disused Hebrew Cemetery near Penzance Station.

One man who did know the Lemon Hart connection was Arthur Caddick who for many years was the Poet Laureate of Cornish inns. Arthur was the author of one of our very first Bossiney titles in 1973: *Broadsides from Bohemia*: 'In praise of Painters, publicans and other Cornish Saints.'

OLD NEWLYN on the edge of Mount's Bay where the British Fleet came to shelter after the Battle of Trafalgar.

Here is a poem from that early Bossiney publication:

A FOUNTAIN OF LATE HONOUR

This Kingdom's sombre twilight
Dims splendours one by one –
It's a rum go, my handsomes,
A rum go . . . it's gone!
That rum which banished blizzards,
Or the doldrums, from the gizzards
Of a fleet that dared all hazards
For duty to be done.
A weeping Bosun ends his log:
"Mainbrace scuppered – no more Grog!"

Jack shall be no longer jolly,

Tars turn black with melancholy –
Oh! lament Trafalgar day!

Penzance of ancient Charter,
Rich lode of Cornish fame,
I hurl reproaches at you,
In this your hour of shame!
Why have you shed no lustre
On that merchant of your borough
Who primed Lord Nelson's muster?
'Twas Lemon Hart, his name,
He victualled Rum for all that Fleet –
Might not his name adorn a street?

Would we have won that doom fraught hour
If Lemon Hart had played it sour
Before Trafalgar Day?

O your Worship, O Ye Aldermen,
O Burgesses, the lot,
Could you vote a fountain
For some well-favoured spot,
To spout rich Rum for you and me
And scent your townsman's memory?
How are things in Demerara?
Perhaps they'd pay the scot
If your Committee, plus Town Clerk,
Went to woo their beauties dark.

If not, levy a Bacchic Rate
So One & All may celebrate
Lemon Hart's Trafalgar Day!

If we come up into Cornwall to Camborne and Redruth we are in the heart of the old mining country. Here we encounter a curious tale of industrial relations. Boulton, the Birmingham ironmaster who installed Watt's engines in the tin mines, saved the mining industry and then incredibly caused its catastrophic downfall. Insisting on charging royalties on the working of his pumps by the hour he provoked the fury of the mine owners – the greatest of whom was Sir Francis Basset of Tehidy, owner of the Great Dolcoath Mine – who refused to pay. They closed the mines and 'threw the miners on the parish'. The miners, in turn, revolted not against Sir Francis Basset and the other owners but against Boulton. It was another October day: October 1787 and the miners marched down the cobbled streets, but Boulton was ready for them. Bush telegraph had warned him. There was no going to arbitration in 1787. Boulton met them with musket in his hand and backed by a brace of light field pieces, loaded and primed. Not a shot was fired – the crowd dispersed – and nobody was hurt.

Let us go south for our next odd story, to Helston. Henry Trengrouse was the man who 'thought of' the breeches buoy for saving the lives of sailors while watching men die off Loe Pool from a wrecked vessel. The buoy became a great success. Between the calendars 1870 and 1920 it was the means of saving ten thousand lives. And Henry Trengrouse's reward? The only reward he ever got for this important invention was fifty pounds, from the Board of Trade, as expenses, a silver medal from the Royal Society of Arts and a diamond ring from Alexander I of Russia. 'My country first,' cried the Cornishman. He died penniless.

Would you expect to find an inn without a bar?

'Certainly not!' would probably be the reply. But, in fact, there is such an hostelry in Cornwall. Well, almost such an hostelry. At the Punch Bowl at Lanreath the bars have always been referred to as 'kitchens'. Here, for example, you'll find the Visitors' Kitchen and the Farmers' Kitchen. When Fowey was a bustling port in the 1700s, coaches would have stopped at the Punch Bowl for refreshment for both passengers and horses. Standing opposite the lovely old church, it has long been well-known for its food and drink and has always been a central part of the village's life and times, serving as a courthouse in the days when it was a busier village.

The inn sign here is interesting, designed in the 1950s by the painter Augustus John. He was a friend of the landlord and a frequent visitor. One family kept the Punch Bowl for close on 200 years. They were the Leans who, up to 1867, ran two establishments. Eventually, Noah Lean, the father, who had bought the

THE MONUMENT to Sir Francis Basset high above the mining country of Camborne and Redruth.

THE PUNCH BOWL sign at Lanreath designed by painter Augustus John.

Punch Bowl from Lieutenant General F.W. Buller, bought the White Horse from his son for £65 and the two merged.

To explore the history of our Cornish inns is a means of uncovering a mine of social history. It's been said 'that every church has something to say . . .' The same is true of our pubs. Equally our Cornish churches have more than their fair share of curiosity and oddity.

THE BEAUTIFUL, but treacherous coastline near Tintagel – the Iota went down not far from this spot.

ST ENODOC Church, photographed in the 1970s.

Young Catanese Domenico's grave in Tintagel Churchyard is marked by a simple wooden cross and a lifebelt from *The Iota.* Thereby hangs an extraordinary tale. Late one December afternoon in 1893, an Italian ship, *The Iota,* shuddered to her death in a driving snow storm and howling gale. She was on her way from Cardiff to the West Indies, carrying a cargo of coal and a crew of twelve: eleven men and a boy. One seaman attempted to save the boy, Catanese Domenico, by swimming with him for the shore but perished in the bounding, crashing sea. Two others managed to scramble on to the craggy form of Lye Rock but had little hope of survival without help. It came in the form of three local men volunteering, aided by a coast-guard. In darkness the four Cornishmen succeeded in getting on to the rock and, not understanding a word of Italian, reassured the two seamen by clasping their hands. It was then discovered that the remaining seven Italians were on a ledge, lower down, not far above the angry sea. One man, Charles Hambly, courageously worked his way down to them and miraculously one by one they were brought up and transported to safety by the coastguard's cradle.

Finally, on this postscript expedition, let us go to St Enodoc Church. It has a beautiful but curious position: between the tenth and thirteenth hole on St Enodoc golf course.

Here, standing by the churchyard, facing the Atlantic, it is hard to appreciate that once, that lovely open sea over Daymer Bay was a forest inhabited by wild animals. Moreover, this is no pure speculation, for in 1857 a fierce Atlantic gale moved the sands to such an extent stumps and roots of trees and the horns and teeth of animals were exposed. But before long the sands hid them again, and today we have to use our imagination.

St Enodoc Church, with its little spire pointing like a crooked finger into the sky, began life some seven hundred years ago. It has suffered badly at the hands of nature. Early in the 1880s the adjoining commons were nothing more than shifting sands and the church was so buried that, at one stage, in order to keep the tithes, the parson and his loyal clerk had to be lowered through a skylight for the only service of the year!

The restoration of St Enodoc took place during 1863-64. Yet oddly enough only a quarter of a century ago, a well-known Cornish painter told me how, one afternoon, she had gone for a walk in North Cornwall, and had come across an old church buried in the sands. Her recollection of the experience was so detailed that she sent me a written account of the strange events of that afternoon – reading her report suggested she had encountered St Enodoc Church in the early 1800s. When I told her so, she confirmed two friends, who had heard her verbal recollection and later read her writing on the subject, said immediately: 'That would have been St Enodoc as it was!'

I was, at the time, researching material for my first supernatural book. Though she had been happy to talk about the incident at length, and to write in detail, the painter refused me permission to publish her story. She did not want the publicity, maybe even feared ridicule. Twenty five years ago, there was a great deal of cynicism –

much of it cruel – on the subject of paranormal possibility. Anyway, though the lady in question has passed on to the great studio in the sky, I continue to respect her confidence – and merely give the outline.

Did she genuinely travel back in time? Or was it a kind of dream – some form of sleep walking perhaps?

Now we shall never know. Nevertheless it remains a fascinating area of speculation and perhaps the right note on which to end *Curious Cornwall.*

TURBULENT SEAS with spray and spume breaking over Trebetherick Cliffs.

Author's Acknowledgements:

THE AUTHOR wishes to thank the various people who talked to him about their subjects. Thanks also to the illustrators Ray Bishop and Felicity Young, who have done so much for Bossiney over the years, and Alex Gardiner, making his Bossiney debut, who photographed the Romany Museum and the Broomfield Horse Sanctuary.

He is also indebted to Sally Dodd for typing the manuscript and her help in tracking down some rare old picture postcards, Maggie Ginger for her continuing work as cover designer and last, but not least, Angela Larcombe for her thoughful editing.

MORE BOSSINEY BOOKS . . .

MYSTERIES IN THE CORNISH LANDSCAPE

by **Tamsin Thomas** of Radio Cornwall

A tour of thirty historic locations in Cornwall by the well-known Cornish broadcaster, starting at Chun Castle down in the Hundred of Penwith and ending at The Hurlers on the eastern edge of Bodmin Moor.

'Tamsin takes us on an enjoyable and speculative canter – literally for she is often on horseback – through these fascinating and often controversial features of old Kernow.'

Donald Rawe, Cornish Scene

'Tamsin has produced a delightful book which will enchant her audience.'

Ronnie Hoyle, The Western Morning News

AROUND & ABOUT THE SMUGGLERS' WAYS

by **David Mudd**

Working through almost forty different sources, including the records of H.M. Customs & Excise itself, David Mudd (who discovered in the course of his research that his great-grandfather was a Customs officer) has produced a book that is as heady and addictive as the spirits, the wines and the tobaccos that once followed fish, tin and copper as Cornwall's great industries. Several of the sketches and many of the photographs are by David's wife, Diana.

'... scrapes the romantic glitter from Cornwall's erstwhile illicit trade ... Meticulously researched and written in David Mudd's lively factual style it makes absorbing reading.'

Alison Poole, Leader Group of Newspapers

DAPHNE DU MAURIER COUNTRY

by **Martyn Shallcross**

A special look at Cornwall in which the internationally-famous novelist set important stories.

'A treasure chest for those who love Cornwall and the du Maurier novels.'

Valerie Mitchell, The Packet Group of Newspapers

SUPERSTITION AND FOLKLORE

by **Michael Williams**

A survey of Westcountry Superstitions: interviews on the subject and some Cornish and Devon folklore.

'... the strictures that we all ignore at our peril. To help us to keep out of trouble, Mr Williams has prepared a comprehensive list.'

Frank Kempe, North Devon Journal-Herald

MORE BOSSINEY BOOKS . . .

KING ARTHUR COUNTRY in CORNWALL, THE SEARCH for the REAL ARTHUR

by **Brenda Duxbury, Michael Williams** and **Colin Wilson**
Over 50 photographs and 3 maps
An exciting exploration of the Arthurian sites in Cornwall and Scilly, including the related legends of Tristan and Iseult, with The Search for the Real Arthur by Colin Wilson.
'*. . . provides a refreshing slant on an old story linking it with the present.*'
Caroline Righton, The Packet Newspapers

SUPERNATURAL SEARCH IN CORNWALL

by **Michael Williams**

DISCOVERING BODMIN MOOR

by **E.V. Thompson**

PARANORMAL IN THE WESTCOUNTRY

by **Michael Williams**

MOUNT'S BAY

by **Douglas Williams**

WEST CORNWALL CAMERA

by **Douglas Williams** – photographs by Harry Penhaul

ABOUT LAND'S END

by **Wendy Lewis**

CASTLES OF CORNWALL

by **Mary & Hal Price**

THE RIVER TAMAR

by **Sarah Foot**

We shall be pleased to send you our catalogue giving full details of our growing list of titles for Devon, Cornwall, Dorset, Somerset and Wiltshire and forthcoming publications. If you have difficulty in obtaining our titles, write direct to Bossiney Books, Land's End, St Teath, Bodmin, Cornwall.